real U

3
YA

GUIDE TO

LIVING ON YOUR OWN

LIESA ABRAMS

Real U Guides

Publisher and CEO:
Steve Schultz

Editor-in-Chief:
Megan Stine

Art Director:
C.C. Krohne

Illustration:
Mike Strong

Production Manager:
Alice Todd

Copy Editor:
Leslie Fears

Editorial Assistant:
Gabriel A. Wildau

Library of Congress Control Number: 2004090909

ISBN: 0-9744159-8-7

First Edition
10 9 8 7 6 5 4 3 2 1

Published by
Real U, Inc.
2582 Centerville Rosebud Rd.
Loganville, GA 30052

www.realuguides.com

Real U is a trademark of Real U, Inc.

Photo Credits:
Cover and Page 1: David Sacks/Getty Images; Page 3: ArtToday;
Page 4: Digital Vision/Getty Images; Page 5: Dirty dishes, Michael
Matisse/Getty Images; Sandwich, C Squared Studios/Getty Images;
Visitors in doorway, Pando Hall/Getty Images; Suds in washing
machine, Janis Christie/Getty Images; Girl reading with vacuum
cleaner, Digital Vision/Getty Images; Page 6: Couple cooking,
Photodisc Collection/Getty Images; Sandwich, C Squared
Studios/Getty Images; Page 7: Rumpled bedding, ArtToday;
Flyswatter, ArtToday; Page 8: Girl with shopping bags, Donna
Day/Getty Images; Phone, ArtToday; Page 9: Digital Vision/Getty
Images; Page 10: Britt Erlanson/Getty Images; Page 11: Digital
Vision/Getty Images; Page 12: Wooden spoon, ArtToday; White
utensil set, ArtToday; Page 13: Kale in strainer, ArtToday;
Red and yellow bowls, ArtToday; Pot with wooden spoon,
ArtToday; Page 14: ArtToday; Page 15: Microwave, ArtToday;
China plate, ArtToday; Page 16: Ryan McVay/Getty Images;
Page 17: Quiche, Greg Kuchik/Getty Images; Ravioli dinner,
Steve Schultz; Page 18: Salmon dish, Steve Schultz; Dinner party,
Ryan McVay/Getty Images; Page 20: Folded laundry in basket,
Janis Christie/Getty Images; Guy in laundromat, Thinkstock/Getty
Images; Page 21: RubberBall Productions/Getty Images; Page 22:
Megan Stine; Page 23: Suds in washing machine, Janis
Christie/Getty Images; Shampoo, Photodisc Collection/Getty
Images; Page 24: Doug Menuez/Getty Images; Page 25: ArtToday;
Page 27: Woman pulling sheets out of dryer, ArtToday; Guy on
cellphone in laundromat, Thinkstock/Getty Images; Page 28: Guy
ironing, Megan Stine; Clothes hangers, ArtToday; Page 29:
ArtToday; Page 30: Pando Hall/Getty Images; Page 31: ArtToday;
Page 32: Photodisc Collection/Getty Images; Page 33: Michael
Matisse/Getty Images; Page 34: ArtToday; Page 35: ArtToday;
Page 36: Biting Electrical Cord, Tim Jones/Getty Images; Fixing
the sink, Phil Boorman/Getty Images; Page 37: RubberBall
Productions/Getty Images; Page 38: Toilet Hookup, Megan Stine;
Flooded Sign, Photo 24/Getty Images; Page 40: Woman fixing sink
in jeans, Greg Ceo/Getty Images; Gas Stove, ArtToday; Page 41:
David Buffington/Getty Images; Page 42: Photolink/Getty Images;
Page 43: Circuit breakers, Megan Stine; Man switching circuit
breakers, Megan Stine; Page 44: Barry Yee/Getty Images; Page 45:
Ryan McVay/Getty Images; Page 46: Jana Leon/Getty Images;
Page 47: Vladimir Pcholkin/Getty Images; Page 48: C Squared
Studios/Getty Images; Page 49: ArtToday; Page 50: ArtToday;
Page 51: Sailboats, ArtToday; Gym scene, ArtToday; Page 52:
Digital Vision/Getty Images; Page 53: Ryan McVay/Getty Images;
Page 54: Women's feet, Tim Hall/Getty Images; Couple at dinner,
ArtToday; Page 55: ArtToday; Page 56: RubberBall
Productions/Getty Images; Page 57: Jim Arbogast/Getty Images;
Page 58: Pando Hall/Getty Images; Page 59: Two men on steps,
Tim Hall/Getty Images; Female friends in city at night, Digital
Vision/Getty Images; Three friends in café window, Digital
Vision/Getty Images; Page 60: ArtToday; Page 61: Comstock
Images/Getty Images; Page 62: Close-up of three girls at party,
Jim Arbogast/Getty Images; Camcorder portrait, Peter Cade/Getty
Images; Page 63: Four people drink from blue cups, Digital
Vision/Getty Images; Birthday cake, C Squared Studios/Getty
Images; Taking picture of group, Ryan McVay/Getty Images.

3

realU

realU

GUIDE TO

LIVING ON YOUR OWN

LIESA ABRAMS

REAL U GUIDE TO LIVING ON YOUR OWN

You're finally on your own . . .

At last. You've got your own place, and now you get to make the rules. If you want to party all night, leave your towels on the bathroom floor, and eat applesauce right out of the jar, no one's going to stop you.

But guess what? No one's going to clean it up when your toilet overflows, either. Or call the landlord when the stove breaks. Or clean out the cabinets when your cereal turns out to be a vacation destination for an army of ants.

Yep, that's right, living on your own isn't all pizza for breakfast and the freedom to hog the remote to your heart's content. When something goes wrong, it's up to you to make the next move. But if you're already starting to freak over the dust bunnies that won't quit or the bills that just keep piling up, hang on...because everything you need to know to have a stress-free life on your own is right here in this guide.

So hit pause on the "meltdown" button, turn the page, and read on.

And Welcome to

real U

TABLE OF CONTENTS

ARE YOU A
DOMESTIC GURU?

You're standing in the middle of your living room, looking around at all the boxes you're about to unpack, thinking how this is the life. Already picking out a new large screen TV for the bedroom? Dreaming of an all-night rager? Take this quiz first to find out if you're really ready to be the master of your domain . . .

1.

Your friend pokes her head in your kitchen and asks if you've got anything she can throw together for a light meal. You tell her no problem, she can help herself to:

A. Her choice of leftover shrimp fried rice, Famous Ray's pepperoni pizza, or chicken vindaloo. Um, maybe not the vindaloo, actually— that might be a little moldy since it's from a couple weeks ago.

B. A delicious combo of peanut butter, Ritz crackers, and mini white chocolate chips.

C. Any of the staples you keep around—eggs and frozen veggies for an omelet, dry pasta and jars of tomato sauce, or canned soup.

these used to be white →

2.

You wash your sheets and pillowcases:

A. Whenever you spill something on them, or about once a month

B. Wait—you're supposed to wash your sheets??

C. Once a week, or once every other week when you're super busy.

3.

You spot something that bears an uncanny resemblance to a roach scamper across your kitchen floor. It's all good—you have a plan of attack. Step one involves:

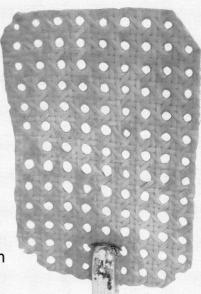

A. Making a pleading phone call to your friend for help—from your safe perch standing on top of the kitchen table.

B. Cleaning off the pesticides shelves at your local drugstore and emptying the bottles into every crevice of your apartment until you can barely breathe.

C. Stomping the roach in sight, and then doing a careful investigation to see if it's got any friends, so you can call an exterminator if necessary.

just got paid!

4.

It's payday—woohoo! The first thing you do after you've got that check in your hands is:

A. Cash it and get ready for an exciting weekend out to make up for last week, which you spent eating cup-o-noodles for dinner every night and watching reruns on TV after your checking account balance dropped to 4 cents.

B. Deposit it and immediately order that leather couch you've been dying for. The bills aren't due until the end of the month, so it's no biggie.

C. Deposit it and withdraw your spending money for the next week, based on the budget you worked out when you landed the apartment.

5.

Time to program the speed-dial on your new phone. Who gets the top three spots?

A. #1 is your parents at home, #2 is your dad's cell, and #3 is your mom's work number.

B. Program the speed dial? What do you mean "program?" You're going to have to call home to find out how this thing works.

C. #1 is your best friend, #2 is your sister, and #3 is the building's super in case you have any major problems.

SO, **ARE** YOU A DOMESTIC GURU?

SCORING

Give yourself one point for every "c" answer.

4-5 POINTS

You're just oozing responsibility. But don't forget to ease up on yourself once in a while—make a mental note of all the time-saving tips in this book so you can free yourself up to have some fun in your new place.

2-3 POINTS

You're on your way to independent living, but you need a little jumpstart to really take you there. Don't worry—you'll have all the inspiration you need when you get your first month's bills!

0-1 POINTS

Uh-oh—is it too late to get that security deposit back? You're in need of an attitude adjustment, stat, unless you want to end up back at Mom and Dad's house in the very near future. But read on, and you'll be scoring big points on the Independence-O-Meter sooner than you think!

COOKING 101:

A REAL U
CRASH COURSE

Let's face it—if you're still getting used to living on your own, you're probably not whipping up gourmet meals every night of the week.

But you've gotta eat, and believe it or not, the day will come when you can't stomach one more egg roll or slice of pizza. So it's time to get friendly with your microwave and find out what else it can do—other than produce mass quantities of theater-style real butter more-salt-and-fat-than-your-minimum-weekly-allowance popcorn. (Can anyone say broccoli?)

You might even want to invite some friends over and impress them with a totally delicious any-idiot-can-make-it home-cooked meal. Here are some basics that'll help you start using your kitchen as more than just a place to store the leftover takeout.

Watch the fingers!

KITCHEN ESSENTIALS:

18 THINGS EVERY KITCHEN NEEDS

One peek at a foodie catalog or one click on a housewares web site, and you'll be convinced you need everything from an avocado peeler to an egg separator to an ice cream machine before your kitchen is complete. But before you go into massive debt over that espresso machine, check out this bare bones list of basics.

TOOLS OF THE TRADE

- 2-quart saucepan with cover for small tasks like boiling rice, heating soup, and steaming broccoli
- 10- or 12-inch skillet or sauté pan
- 4-quart pot for boiling spaghetti and making big batches of home-made soup
- Set of 2 or 3 nested microwave-safe mixing bowls. These can double as serving bowls for salad and vegetables.
- 2-cup liquid Pyrex measuring cup
- Set of dry measuring cups
- Set of measuring spoons
- Wooden spoon
- Pancake turner

- Set of knives—a paring knife, a serrated knife, and a chef's knife for chopping and carving
- Strainer or colander
- Tongs
- Baking sheet
- 9" pie plate
- Large baking pan, 13 x 9 x 2", for lasagna and Rice Krispie treats. This can double as a roasting pan in a pinch.
- Can opener/bottle opener
- Potholders
- Soup ladle

EXTRAS IT WOULD BE NICE TO HAVE...

- Tea kettle
- 9x9 square pan
- Meat thermometer
- Rubber spatula
- Grater
- Corkscrew

HOW LONG DO I NUKE IT?

If you have to call home every time you need to warm up a blueberry muffin, thaw a ground beef patty, or reheat a plate of spaghetti, you're going to need a monster cell phone plan with lots of free minutes. Or you could check out this chart with guidelines for thawing, heating, and reheating some basic foods. Remember that exact timing can vary depending on the microwave, so start at the low end of the range and then keep nuking it until it's thawed or hot.

COOK

Half a pound of fresh asparagus: **2 to 4 minutes on high,** covered with plastic wrap.

One pound of fresh broccoli: **6 to 8 minutes on high,** covered with plastic wrap.

One large Idaho potato: **7 minutes on high.** Pierce with a fork first, and turn the potato over halfway through the cooking time.

Hot dog: **30 to 40 seconds on high,** covered with a paper towel.

WARM OR REHEAT

One slice of leftover pizza: **30 to 45 seconds on high, if it came from the fridge. 1 to 2 minutes on high if it was in the freezer.** (You might want to use a toaster oven for reheating pizza or anything with a crust, since microwaves tend to make bread products soggy or tough. Of course, if your pizza is already soggy and tough, consider trying a different pizzeria!)

Blueberry muffin or Danish: **10 to 15 seconds on high.** This is a great way to bring stale baked goods back to life. Works well with day-old glazed doughnuts, too.

Pasta or leftover spaghetti: **45 to 90 seconds on high,** in a bowl, covered with a paper towel to prevent splattering.

One piece of leftover chicken: **40 to 60 seconds on high,** covered with a paper towel.

Butter: **8 to 12 seconds on high,** to soften a whole stick of butter from the fridge.

THAW

1 lb of frozen ground meat: **3 to 5 minutes, using the defrost setting.** Watch carefully, and when the meat is partially thawed—halfway through the time—cut the whole lump in half and rotate the two halves so that the frozen "inside" section is now on the outside. This will prevent cooking the edges while the inside is still frozen.

Frozen Boneless chicken breast: **5 to 7 minutes, using the defrost setting.** Turn chicken over halfway through.

Frozen pastries or bagels: **40 to 60 seconds on defrost.**

NUKING NO-NO'S

Microwaves are one of those inventions that make you wonder how anyone lived without them. But don't get carried away—there are definitely limits to what you can and should put in yours. You probably already know that you should never put anything metal in the microwave, but here are some other things you should never nuke:

- One-time use containers like margarine tubs, takeout cartons, etc.

- Anything with gold or metallic trim, including fine china with gold trim, which can melt in the microwave.

- Ordinary glass, such as glass plates, drinking glasses, empty mayo jars and such. Pyrex is o.k.

- Plastic, paper, or Tupperware pieces that aren't marked microwave safe.

- Nothing. Never use the microwave as a timer! Anytime you use the microwave, make sure there's something inside.

don't put grandma's china in the microwave!

IS IT SAFE?

To find out for sure whether a dish is microwave safe, use this simple test: Put the dish in the microwave by itself, along with a microwave safe container holding water. Set the microwave for one minute—no longer! At the end of the minute, the cup of water should be hot. If the other container isn't hot, it's safe to use. (Don't try this with your great-grandmother's tea set, however—unless you totally hate the pattern and are trying to get rid of it. Do you really think a 100-year-old cream pitcher was meant to be nuked?)

CAN'T COOK? FAKE IT!
3 GREAT MEALS ANYONE CAN MAKE

How did this happen?
Somehow in your excitement to invite
everyone you know over to see your new
place, you blanked on the fact that you're
supposed to feed people when you tell
them to show up at 7:00 on a Friday night.

But hey—no problem. You won't have to serve up
the Kraft Mac 'n' Cheese you've been munching for
the past two weeks. We've got some real meals that even a
total kitchen geek can whip up to impress his or her friends.

RAVIOLI WITH BROWNED BUTTER AND SAGE

This is, hands down, the easiest gourmet dish you'll ever make. If you can boil water, you can nail this recipe. Serve with a mixed green salad topped with orange slices and dried cranberries, and your friends will think you're the next Emeril.

Ingredients:

1 package mushroom or cheese ravioli, fresh, from the refrigerator case at the grocery store

3 Tablespoons butter

6-8 fresh sage leaves

Directions:

Cook the ravioli in 2 quarts of salted, boiling water, according to the directions on the package. Hint: put 1 tablespoon vegetable oil in the water before adding the pasta. The oil keeps the pasta from sticking together.

While the ravioli are cooking, prepare the browned butter sauce. Melt the butter over medium low heat in a large skillet or frying pan, and sauté the sage leaves in it until crisp. Continue cooking, swirling the pan and watching the butter until it begins to turn golden brown. Remove from heat when the butter is browned, but not burned.

Drain the ravioli when they are almost cooked. Slip them into the frying pan with the browned butter and sage sauce, to coat them well. Serves 2-3.

SUNDAY BRUNCH QUICHE

You're a grownup, right? So forget about frozen pancakes slathered in syrup out of a bottle shaped like a woman. Try this quick and easy recipe for a delicious Sunday brunch. Serve the quiche with a bowl of fresh fruit salad, some warmed French bread, and a pitcher of Mimosas to impress your guests with a simple yet sophisticated meal.

Ingredients:

One 9" Prepared Pie Crust

4 eggs, beaten

1 cup milk

2 Tablespoons finely chopped onions

1/2 teaspoon salt

2 Tablespoons chopped parsley

3 ounces shredded cheddar cheese

3 ounces shredded swiss cheese

3/4 cup broccoli or asparagus, cut into small pieces

Directions:

Preheat oven to 350 degrees.

Combine eggs, milk, onion, salt, and parsley. Whisk with a fork and set aside. Layer the broccoli or asparagus and the cheese in a pie crust-lined pan. Pour egg mixture over broccoli and cheese. Bake for 40-50 minutes, until knife inserted in center comes out clean. Serves 6.

SALMON AND VEGETABLES BAKED IN PARCHMENT

For a fancy-schmancy dinner that will impress and amaze your friends, check out this easy recipe for fish baked in parchment. You'll need to buy baking parchment for this—don't even think about using regular paper, which could catch fire in the oven. If you can't find parchment anywhere, you can get away with aluminum foil. Best part of this recipe? The fact that it leaves you with absolutely nothing to clean up afterwards!

Ingredients:

2 salmon fillets

2 to 3 tablespoons butter, softened

1 large carrot,
peeled and very thinly sliced
(no more than 1/8" thick)

2 small potatoes,
very thinly sliced into 1/8" slices

3 sprigs fresh dill, chopped

salt and pepper

parchment paper

Directions:

Preheat oven to 350 degrees.

Cut two 16" circles out of parchment paper. Spread the entire top of each circle with one tablespoon butter. Put one salmon fillet on each piece of buttered parchment, but don't center it—put it off to the side. Arrange the carrot and potato slices on top of the fish. Dot the top with butter, add the dill, and sprinkle with salt and pepper to taste.

Now fold the parchment in half, enclosing the fish in a semi-circle. Starting at one side, and working your way around the semi-circle of parchment, tightly fold the edges in 1/4" toward the middle. Then fold the paper over again, crimping the edge as you go to form a tight seal.

Carefully slide both packets of fish onto a baking sheet. Bake in the preheated oven for 12-14 minutes, depending on the thickness of the fish. Remove from oven and slide each parchment packet onto a plate. Tear or cut open the paper and enjoy!

WHEN TO TOSS IT:
GUIDE TO PERISHABLES

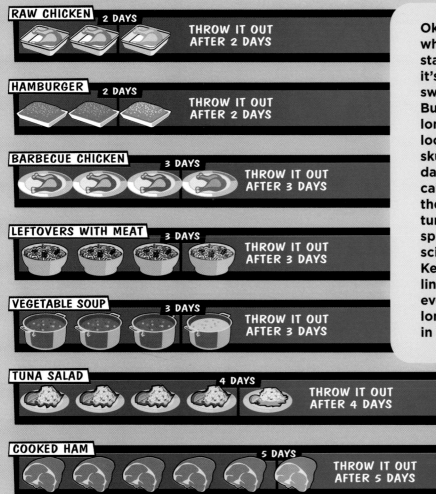

RAW CHICKEN 2 DAYS
THROW IT OUT AFTER 2 DAYS

HAMBURGER 2 DAYS
THROW IT OUT AFTER 2 DAYS

BARBECUE CHICKEN 3 DAYS
THROW IT OUT AFTER 3 DAYS

LEFTOVERS WITH MEAT 3 DAYS
THROW IT OUT AFTER 3 DAYS

VEGETABLE SOUP 3 DAYS
THROW IT OUT AFTER 3 DAYS

Okay, you know that when the Wonder Bread starts growing penicillin, it's time to do a clean sweep of the fridge. But food can go bad long before it starts looking green and skuzzy. In fact, it can be dangerous before you can see, taste, or smell the evidence. So don't turn yourself into a spur-of-the-moment science experiment. Keep these FDA guide-lines in mind if you're ever in doubt about how long to leave something in the fridge.

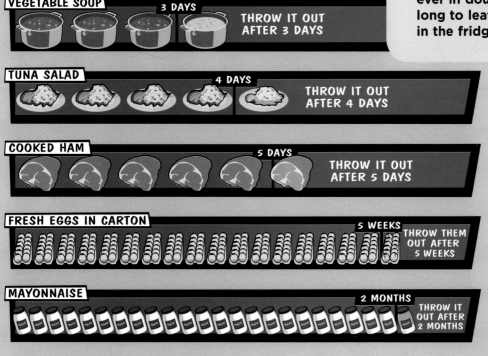

TUNA SALAD 4 DAYS
THROW IT OUT AFTER 4 DAYS

COOKED HAM 5 DAYS
THROW IT OUT AFTER 5 DAYS

FRESH EGGS IN CARTON 5 WEEKS
THROW THEM OUT AFTER 5 WEEKS

MAYONNAISE 2 MONTHS
THROW IT OUT AFTER 2 MONTHS

multi-tasking!

LAUNDRY DAY

If you're tired of shrinking your favorite hoodies or can't afford the huge laundry bills each month from sending your shirts to the cleaners, read on.

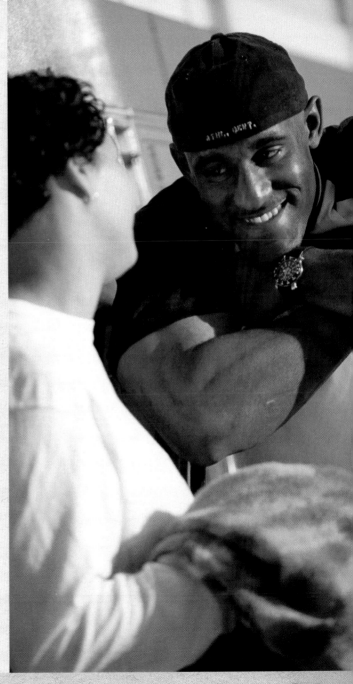

There are lots of ways to get your clothes clean without spending a fortune and ruining half your wardrobe in the process. Hey, it isn't brain surgery—if it were, you'd be getting your clothes messier rather than cleaner!

8 SIMPLE LAUNDRY RULES

1. LEARN TO DECODE THE TAGS ON YOUR CLOTHES.

Every sheet, towel, and piece of clothing you own comes with a tag that tells you the best way to wash and dry the item. Unfortunately, you've got to speak Laundry, not English, to understand it sometimes. Here's a sidebar with a key to the most common symbols. For links to a web site that decodes every care label icon under the sun, visit www.realuguides.com.

2. SORT YOUR LOAD.

Unless you want to be that cliché guy walking around in pink shirts and underwear, sort your laundry by colors because some fabrics bleed or run every time they're washed. Red is usually the culprit, but it's not the only thing that can dye your whites. Vibrant blues can do it, too—especially a new pair of unwashed 501 Levis—and so can blacks, or any fabric that isn't colorfast. Also sort everything according to wash temperatures. And it's a good idea to do a separate pile of terry-cloth towels or robes, and anything made of washable chenille or flannel, since these materials can generate a lot of lint.

Common Care Label Symbols

 Regular Wash

 Hand Wash Only

 Do Not Wash

 Use Normal Cycle Dry

 Do Not Tumble Dry

 Do Not Bleach

 Iron on High Temp

 Iron on Low Temp

 Do Not Iron

 Do Not Dry Clean

too much detergent??

3. CHECK POCKETS FOR TISSUES, MONEY, SCRAPS OF PAPER.

This is totally 101, but it's easy to forget this step when you're in a hurry. Washing a twenty probably won't do much damage—the U.S. government makes cash that lasts! But if you've ever picked tiny shredded pieces of tissue out of your entire load of wet shirts and pants—or seen the look on everyone's face when you yank your confetti-covered clothes out of the dryer at the Laundromat—you know why you don't want to leave stuff in your jeans pocket.

4. PRE-TREAT STAINS.

Once you've sorted your clothes, check for anything that might have a stain you didn't notice when it happened. (For best results, treat stains immediately, not days later.) Soak the stain in detergent or use a spray-on stain remover.

5. DON'T OVERLOAD THE MACHINE.

Proud of yourself for all the moolah you saved by stuffing every single piece of laundry into one load in the washing machine? Think again. When you overload the machine, your clothes don't really move around much, so they don't really come out clean. Don't overdo it on detergent, either—measure out the right amount for the size of your wash load, based on the recommendations of the machine. Too much detergent and you'll have suds stains; too little won't get the job done.

BEST STAIN REMOVER EVER

Grease stains, ink, and chocolate are three of the hardest stains to remove from your clothes. The key to getting them out of a garment that's washable is this: Don't wash it! In fact, once you've put water on a grease stain or ink, your chances of getting it out plummet.

Instead, use a heavy blob of shampoo on the stain, and rub the sides of the fabric together to scrub it out. Don't try this on Dry Clean Only fabrics—only on washables. And don't use a colored shampoo—only clear or golden products. If the stain doesn't seem to come out, add more shampoo. Put a heavy dab on each and every grease stain and treat them all this way. Don't rinse the shampoo out until you're sure the stain is gone. Then wash the garment normally. You'll be amazed at the results!

23

6. CHOOSE THE RIGHT WASH CYCLE.

The wash cycle determines how much agitation your clothes get— or in other words, how rough a ride they have through that water park of a washing machine.

Delicate

You don't want to mangle your fine lingerie or silk boxers, so those things should be washed on the Delicate cycle. Ditto for anything that's sheer, very lightweight, made from lace or loose-knit fabric, or anything with embroidery or fringe. You should also use the Delicate option for anything made of machine-washable silk, wool, acrylic, viscose rayon, or a blend of any of these fibers.

Special note—delicate, small items that could tangle with the rest of the wash, like bras or other lingerie, benefit from being put inside a zippered mesh bag.

Permanent Press

Permanent Press works for most synthetics like polyester, nylon, and blends containing these materials. It's also good for anything formulated to be wrinkle-resistant, including durable-press cotton, linen, and rayon.

Regular

Use the Regular setting for sheets, towels, sturdy whites, heavy-duty jeans, and colorfast cottons and linens (unless they have an anti-wrinkling finish).

Remember that heat can cause shrinkage, whether it's dryer heat or hot water in the washing machine.

7. CHOOSE THE RIGHT WATER TEMPERATURE.

Be careful using hot water on anything that's prone to shrinkage, especially knits or cotton that isn't pre-shrunk. Hot water also increases the chances of color bleeding from one garment to another, so you should avoid using it on bright and dark colors. Hot water does give you the best cleaning, though, and also kills more germs, so try to use hot water for dirty sheets and towels, where sanitizing matters. Warm water works best for permanent press loads, and brights and darks that are colorfast or don't bleed. Choose the cold setting for delicates and any bright or dark fabrics that could bleed or fade.

8. CHOOSE THE RIGHT DRYER SETTINGS.

Before you even put your stuff in the dryer, make sure it belongs there. Some care labels will tell you to "line dry/hang to dry" or "lay flat to dry." If your things are safe in the dryer, just make sure you choose the right heat setting. Opt for low or medium heat for delicates or anything with a high risk of shrinkage. High heat works best for sturdy duds like pre-shrunk jeans and very heavy wet items like towels, which can take a long time to dry. But it's actually a myth that the best result from a dryer is a basket full of piping hot clothes; over-drying isn't good for the fabric. What you really want is to get your items just dry enough. And anything you intend to iron should actually come out of the dryer immediately and slightly damp.

LAUNDRY ON A BUDGET

If you only have the time or cash to do one or two loads of laundry, you can combine things into a few basic loads. The three basic categories are Warm Whites, Cold Darks, and Warm Colors. But you still can't mix red in here (or any item that will bleed), so if you wear a lot of red and hot pink, you're going to need a fourth basic category—Cold Reds. (Isn't that something you sip with nachos and Buffalo wings?)

HOW TO

FOLD FITTED SHEETS

1. Do this activity over a table, couch, or bed, so that the sheet doesn't hang down and touch the floor while you're trying to fold it.

2. Find two corners along one side of the sheet, and slip one hand into each corner.

3. Bring the two hands together, and reverse one corner over the other, so they are nested together.

4. Repeat step three with the other two corners. The sheet is now folded in half, with two corners nested inside two opposite corners.

5. Put one hand in one set of nested corners. Put your other hand in the other set. Bring them together, and once again flip one set of corners over the other. Now you have all four corners nested or tucked inside each other, and the sheet has been folded in half twice.

6. Lay the sheet on the table or bed, with the "open" side of the corners facing up. Straighten out the edges so that they are folded in neatly. Fold the sheet in half again, twice. Voila!

WARNING:

Unless you're lucky enough to have your own washer and dryer, you'll have to use a public Laundromat. Just keep these precautions in mind to make the experience as painless as possible.

Watch out for super hot dryers.

The machines in Laundromats are usually heavy-duty, and often the temperature dial doesn't really work—it's just all hot, all the time. If you choose high heat in a commercial Laundromat, you may be giving your clothes a serious sauna. On the other hand, some commercial dryers seem to run forever without drying your clothes—a clever ploy to get you to keep feeding them quarters. Best plan: Choose low or medium heat for most items and keep checking on your clothes to make sure they're not being shrunk to monkey size or baked to a crisp.

Empty lint filters before you start your dry cycle.

Lint build-up slows down the dryer's effectiveness—meaning you may have to run your load through another cycle, costing more time and quarters. (Just when you thought the dryer was too hot—now it's too slow!) Lint should be scooped out of the lint filters after every load, but don't count on the person before you actually remembering to do it.

Don't abandon your post.

It's tempting to leave the Laundromat for the thirty minutes to an hour that it takes for your clothes to run through a wash or dry cycle, but if you do, you run the risk that someone will remove your clothes if the machine finishes before you return. You don't really want some stranger handling your stuff, do you?

- Bring something to read while you wait, or come with a friend and hang out together while you're getting your clothes clean.

- You could also find a laundry partner (someone you know and trust) and take turns "babysitting" each other's wash while the other one runs errands.

Timing is everything.

Think Sunday afternoon is the perfect time to do your laundry? Yeah, well, so does everyone else—which is why the Laundromat will be crammed when you show up. You'll be stuck waiting for a washer, or worse—you'll get through the washing phase only to be stuck waiting for a free dryer while your wet clothes sit in the basket.

- Try to find a time that works for your schedule but isn't one of the most popular ones at your Laundromat. If you're an early riser or a night owl, take advantage of those windows of time when the Laundromat won't be so overpopulated.

- Many Laundromats have televisions. If there's a weeknight with a primetime lineup you like to watch, you could check it out at the Laundromat while your clothes are being cleaned and free yourself from any couch potato guilt.

HOW TO

IRON A DRESS SHIRT

Most people iron the front of the shirt first and the sleeves last. Big mistake. By the time you get around to the sleeves, you've mangled the shirt on the ironing board so much that the front is wrinkled again!

1. Start with a damp shirt or fill a spray bottle with water to mist the shirt as you work.
2. Check the tag on the shirt to make sure you set the iron to the right temperature.
3. Iron the backs and fronts of sleeves.
4. Iron the back then the front of the collar.
5. Iron the backs and fronts of cuffs.
6. Iron the yoke—the part that goes across your shoulders—and then the back of the shirt, one half at a time.
7. Iron the strip with buttonholes, and the pocket, if there is one (which should be opened).
8. Iron the front of the shirt, one half at a time.
9. Immediately hang the shirt on a hanger, buttoning at least one button.

HOW OFTEN SHOULD YOU DRY CLEAN?

If clothes have stains, smoke, or food odors, clean more often. Otherwise, clean garments after they've been worn a number of times. How many?

Pants ....worn 3x

Sweaters ....worn 6x

Suits ....worn 8x

Winter Coats....once a year

← iron the sleeves first

THE TRUTH ABOUT
DRY CLEANING

Laundry is enough of a pain and expense when you're just dealing with the washing machine. So you're probably doing whatever you can to avoid buying clothes with that dreaded message on the tags— Dry Clean Only. But before you start putting anything with this label back on the rack, check out these tips on how to save on dry cleaning costs.

Shop Around

Your first instinct is probably to go with the cleaner that's closest to your apartment. But resist the impulse and spend an afternoon checking out the other dry cleaners in your neighborhood. Compare prices to see where you can get the best deals, and ask if they'll give you a discount for prepaying your order when you drop your clothes off.

Ask for a Deal

Never assume you can't bargain. If you do find a better deal at a dry cleaner's that's really inconvenient, try going to the one closer to your home and asking if they're willing to match the deal the other guy's giving you. If you can provide steady business, there's a chance you'll get what you're looking for.

Most cleaners offer discounts if you're cleaning enough items, like a reduced cost per shirt if you clean a certain number of shirts, or if you bring a pair of pants along with the shirts. Try to save up your dirty clothes for one trip a month instead of bringing smaller bundles more frequently.

An Alternative to Dry Cleaning

Pay attention to whether your garment says Dry Clean *Only*. If it doesn't say "only" you may be able to clean it another way. For instance, sometimes delicate natural fabrics like silk, wool, or cashmere can be washed by hand with a mild product like Woolite.

Even labels that insist you should only dry-clean don't have to mean a trip to the cleaners. You could also try Dryel, a product that allows you to clean your Dry Clean Only or "hand-wash only" clothes in a special bag inside a dryer. The box comes with complete instructions to take you through the process, and it's safe for most special fabrics except for leather, velvet, fur, or suede. Stick to the professionals for anything made of these fabrics, anything too big to fit into the Dryel bag, or any garment that's very badly stained. Stains will set if you put a garment in the dryer without removing the stain first, or if you try to remove it unsuccessfully.

CLEAN SWEEP:

HOW TO KEEP YOUR APARTMENT LOOKING GREAT

The thing about cleaning your apartment is that it's a trade-off: You do a little work now, so that later you don't have to spend six hours looking for your keys under three months' accumulation of dust and empty pizza boxes.

Or you can think of it this way: wash your tub today, your girlfriend won't report you to the Health Department tomorrow.

But don't worry—keeping your new pad neat doesn't have to take forever and make you want to move back home where someone else is in charge of the vacuum cleaner. In fact, with these helpful housekeeping hints, you'll have plenty of time to enjoy your apartment, fight with your girlfriend over something other than bathroom issues—or find your keys, if you manage to lose them anyway.

ready for guests!

You'll save yourself time if you keep duplicate cleaning supplies in different rooms.

Practice preventive maintenance.

Here's one time when avoiding the problem is actually a great tactic! Spray a tile cleaner in your shower for thirty seconds after your shower every day, and you won't face scary mildew build-up. (Be careful if you have pets—some products are toxic.) Also, take off your shoes when you walk into the apartment—and encourage close friends and family members to do the same—to spare your floor or carpet. Designate certain areas for eating, and keep all food away from the rest of your house, since food is a major contributor to mess.

Buy doubles

It may cost a few extra bucks up front, but you'll save yourself time if you keep duplicate cleaning supplies in different rooms, so you don't have to carry everything around with you. This is especially helpful if your place has stairs. (Who wants to spend all day running up and down the steps to grab a sponge or a bottle of cleaning fluid?) Remember that you're not really losing money on the deal, because you won't run out of toilet bowl cleaner for twice as long, which is a nice time-saving bonus all by itself.

Get literal—and really clean your house from top to bottom.

As in, start out cleaning the highest surfaces or objects in a room and then keep going down until you finish with sweeping or vacuuming the floor. That way you're not creating extra work for yourself. If you sweep the floor before you dust, you'll just have to sweep all over again when you're done dusting! Also try the inside-out approach: Start by cleaning something like a cabinet or refrigerator from the inside and then move to the outside. Do dry cleaning, like dusting and sweeping, before wet cleaning like mopping.

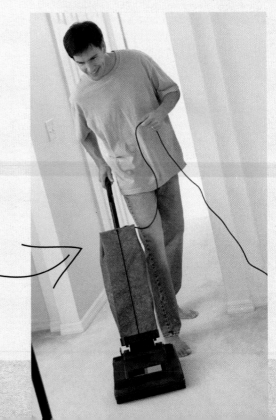

vacuum after dusting, not before

WHAT TO DO WHEN

The key to not feeling overwhelmed about housekeeping is to remember that you don't have to do everything all the time. In fact, some of the major cleaning jobs don't need to be done more than once a year! Here's a breakdown of how often you need to tackle these basic chores.

Daily or every other day	Weekly	Once or twice a month	Once or twice a year
Wash dishes— or run dishwasher if you're lucky enough to have one!	Wipe down sinks and counters in kitchen and bathroom.	Do a thorough cleaning of kitchen and bathroom—including tub and toilet, oven and stove.	Clean out refrigerator.
Make bed.	Wash and change sheets. Do laundry.		
Neaten/tidy by keeping loose papers and mail organized.	Sweep floor and/or vacuum carpet in areas with more traffic or mess.	Vacuum all carpets; sweep and clean floors.	Move heavy furniture (with help!) and clean behind it.
	Quickly dust surface areas.	Dust furniture and items in view.	Polish furniture.
		Clean mirrors and electronics.	Clean lights, light fixtures, pictures, and walls. Wash windows.
Empty the garbage.	Take out recyclables and clean out trash cans with disinfectant spray.		Sort through all your things and give away or throw out anything you're not using. Old clothes that don't fit are in this category, along with expired medications, canned foods, and unwanted gifts.

← don't let the dishes pile up!

33

UNEXPECTED GUESTS?
HOW TO PICK UP YOUR HOUSE IN 15 MINUTES OR LESS

Your cousin just called from his cell phone—he and his girlfriend are in the neighborhood and they want to stop by. You can't exactly say no just because you're a little backlogged on your cleaning, but the sad truth is your place is in no shape for visitors. Don't panic—tell your cousin you can't wait to see him, and then get to work fast.

1. **First, close as many doors as you can.**
   There's no reason your guests have to see your bedroom, for instance. Plan to keep the entertaining in one room—the living room or den—and then shut the doors to any other rooms to keep the mess out of sight.

2. **Next, do some quick neatening.**
   Go through the living room with two trash bags—one to fill with loose garbage that's lying around, and the other to help you quickly pick up and hide your clutter. Stash the bag of good stuff in your bedroom or closet and toss the other bag into the trash. (Preferably not the other way around.)

3. **If there's time, do a quick vacuuming.**
   It will give the room an extra clean feel.

4. **Don't forget the bathroom.**
   Guests may need to make a pit stop. If your tub is in desperate need of bleach, just close the shower curtain or door so no one will be the wiser. Then wipe down the sink with a sponge, and check the toilet—if it's looking scuzzy, dump a little bowl cleaner in and flush. It's better than nothing!

toss it all in the closet!

POST-PARTY STAIN REMOVAL:
WHEN BAD STAINS HAPPEN TO GOOD PEOPLE

As pristine as you keep your home, accidents happen—especially after that mass invasion commonly known as a party. Luckily, this easy guide to stain removal for the most common offenders should help you restore most clothing, carpet, and furniture to its pre-stain glory.

TYPE OF STAIN	REMOVAL TECHNIQUE
Coffee, tea	Rinse/soak in cold water, then use liquid detergent—not soap—to clean remainder.
Wine and other alcoholic beverages	Rinse/soak in cold water and detergent, not soap. For red wine, pour salt on the stain immediately and let it sit, or try blotting stain with club soda.
Oil/grease (cooking oil, butter, or salad dressing)	Never use water first! For washable fabrics and surfaces, dab with shampoo and rub. Only rinse after the grease is removed.
Candle wax	Place paper towel over wax and press gently with warm iron. Wax should come up. If any color from the candle remains, treat with stain remover and then wash.
Chewing gum	Freeze gum with an ice-cube, then break off gum from fabric. Rub any remaining stain with detergent.
Blood	Rinse with cold water—never hot—right away. If the stain has dried, brush away whatever you can, and then soak remaining stain in cold water and detergent.

DEALING WITH CARPET STAINS

When food or drink is spilled on a carpet, you've got to act fast. First blot up the spill, using plain white paper towels (not printed paper towels) until you've absorbed as much of the spill as possible. Then visit www.carpet-rug.com for specific instructions on removing various kinds of stains. Many spills can be treated with plain water or a mild water and liquid dishwashing soap solution, but consult the web site before proceeding. When cleaning a carpet stain, do not scrub as this can ruin the pile. Never pour water onto the carpet! Use dry white paper towels to blot up all the moisture once the stain is removed.

I fixed it!

HANDYMAN

If you're incredibly, blissfully lucky, you will never have a single experience with a clogged drain, blown fuse, cockroach invasion, or any other common household problem.

For the other 99.9% of you, here's a handy guide to how things work around your home, and what to do when something doesn't work the way it's supposed to. For anything major, you should always call your super or landlord, if you're a renter. If you're a homeowner, call in a pro.

And speaking of the pros...guess what one of the biggest differences is between you and them? They know where to find all the important stuff in your apartment. So if you want to get a jump on handling major crises, the first thing you should do when you move into a new place is to locate things like the circuit breaker box, main water shut-off valve, and all the individual water shut-off valves for your sinks, toilets, and tubs.

Read on to find out more...

what does he know that you don't?

WATER, WATER, EVERYWHERE:
HOW TO STOP A FLOOD

It's one thing when you leave the tub running and it overflows all over the floor. Everyone knows what to do about that—cry like a baby, right? And then turn the water off, grab 16 towels, and start mopping it up.

But what if a pipe bursts? Or a hose to the dishwasher breaks?

Whether it's coming from a burst pipe or an overflowing toilet, water gushing across your floor is always a scary sight. But there are a number of ways to stop the flooding, even if they are just temporary fixes while you wait for the plumber to come help.

MAIN WATER SHUTOFF.

Your home has one central water shutoff that will stop all the water flow into your pipes. If you live in an apartment building, there's probably a shutoff for the whole building that you may not be able to control yourself. In a house, the main shutoff is usually in the basement right where the water pipe comes through the wall, from the street. In warmer climates, it might be outside the house, also right where the water pipe enters the house. If you need to turn off all the water in your house, find that knob and turn the wheel clockwise.

the water shutoff for the toilet

INDIVIDUAL WATER SHUTOFFS.

It's more likely, however, that you'll face an overflowing toilet or similar disaster in which you just need to stop the water coming from one fixture. In that case, look for the individual shutoffs to faucets and to appliances that use water, like a washing machine. If you ever need to turn these off, check under or next to faucets, and search the pipes around appliances until you find the shutoff knob. Turn the knob clockwise, just like you do with a main water shutoff.

OVERFLOWING TOILET.

If the water's coming from an overflowing toilet, the fastest way to stop the flow is to take the lid off the tank and pull up on the float ball. Newer toilet mechanisms don't have a float ball—they have a stacked column mechanism with a jutting lever arm. You can stop the water by lifting that arm, but since it's not as immediately obvious how this works, you might want to practice. Take the tank lid off the toilet and then flush it. Watch the mechanism work. Then flush again, and this time gently lift the lever arm, to stop the water from flowing into the bowl.

Of course, if the real thing happens, you'll have gallons of water all over your floor. When cleanup time comes, don't bother wasting all those rolls of paper towels—you'll need real towels to sop up that much water.

FLOODE

HOW TO PLUNGE A TOILET

1

2

WRAP A LARGE TOWEL AROUND THE BASE OF THE TOILET TO SOAK UP ANY POTENTIAL OVERFLOW.

3

SLOWLY LOWER THE PLUNGER INTO THE WATER AT AN ANGLE. PRESS GENTLY AGAINST THE SIDE OF THE BOWL TO EXPEL ANY AIR TRAPPED IN THE PLUNGER CUP.

REMEMBER THAT IT'S WATER PRESSURE, NOT AIR PRESSURE THAT MOVES THE CLOG. AIR PRESSURE ONLY GETS YOU SPLASHED!

4

NOW CAREFULLY MOVE THE PLUNGER CUP TO COVER THE HOLE IN THE BOTTOM OF THE BOWL.
GIVE THE HANDLE A SOLID, FORCEFUL PUSH–BUT SLOWLY TO AVOID SPLASHING.

5

HOLDING THE PLUNGER IN PLACE, REPEAT STEP 4 UNTIL YOU HEAR THE CLOG BEGIN TO MOVE.
TWO OR THREE TIMES SHOULD GET IT GOING!

5 PLUMBING DISASTERS

It's easy to think that any problem with your plumbing is going to mean calling in a professional, pronto, since no one wants to face a flooded apartment. But there are actually some snags that you might be able to fix yourself. Try these first before you pick up the phone.

1. CLOGGED DRAIN IN SINK OR TUB

If there's water in the sink or tub, remove as much as possible. Then slowly pour a large pot of boiling water down the drain. Next, try using a plunger over the drain—yes, even in the sink. Close off the water escape hole with a washcloth, and plunge until you hear the clogged material moving in the pipes. Avoid using commercial drain cleaners, since they can actually hurt the pipes. For regular pipe maintenance, pour a cup of bleach down the drain every couple of weeks.

2. STOPPED-UP TOILET

Don't keep flushing if it's not working, or the toilet will overflow. Most clogged toilets can be unclogged with a plunger if you know the right technique. See the illustrations on Page 39.

GAS LEAKS

The minute you smell gas in your home, the first thing you should do is open all your windows to let fresh air in. (Unless it's just your cousin eating too many burritos again.) Then try to figure out where the smell is coming from. Your gas stove is one obvious choice. If the pilot light has gone out, you can relight it following the instructions that came with the stove. Be extremely careful, however! You don't want to light a match anywhere near a contained build-up of gas. Note—it's not a DIY job if you're already smelling serious gas around the appliance, or if you think the pilot light could have been out for a while.

If you're not sure what's causing the smell—and often even if you are—it's a smart idea to call your local gas company and/or the fire department to come check out the problem. These professionals can help you relight pilot lights, and show you the safe way to do so.

3. JAMMED GARBAGE DISPOSAL

If the disposal is making noise but you can tell that the grinder isn't turning around—or if it's absolutely silent when you flip the switch—it's probably jammed. Turn it off and then try using a broom handle, upside down, to manually rotate the disposal mechanism. Stick the handle in the hole and then "stir" clockwise, turning until you get the mechanism moving again.

4. TOILET TANK WON'T STOP RUNNING

Jiggle the handle, or take the tank lid off and look to see if anything inside has shifted out of its place. Lift up the flush valve and make sure it's placed back down correctly. Often this will do the trick.

5. FROZEN PIPES

If the temperature dips below freezing, your pipes are at risk of freezing and possibly bursting. When you know frigid weather is on the way, open kitchen or bathroom cabinet doors to let warm air reach the pipes, and leave the faucet dripping just a trickle. If this preventive measure fails and your pipes still freeze, search all areas of the pipe leading to the faucet for any frozen spots. (Keep the faucet open, though.) When you find the frozen spot or spots on the pipe, try heating the pipe slowly with a hair dryer.

INFESTATIONS

They're living in your home, eating your food, and they don't even help with the rent. Nope, I'm not talking about your mooch friends—I'm talking about the little creepy crawlies that might invade your kitchen at some point. Depending on where you live, it could be ants, roaches, or another type of buggie.

If you're dealing with ants, the first thing to do is take everything out of your cabinets and spray or squash any bugs in sight. (Make sure you get them all.) Look for holes in your cabinets or floor where the bugs could be finding their way in, and seal up any holes you find, using a foam spray sealant from the hardware store. If you find bugs in your flour or cornmeal, you might want to consider keeping that stuff in the fridge instead of your cabinets, to cut down on future bug visits.

When you've got a serious infestation on your hands, like a problem with cockroaches, you probably need to bring in a professional exterminator. The chemicals used to kill roaches can be fairly strong, however, and some of them are toxic. To protect your health, it might be a good idea to stay away from your home for a day or two while the chemicals do their thing, so have a back-up plan in mind for somewhere to crash. (And don't give the roaches your cell phone number.)

POWER OUTAGES

You're hanging around the house one day, watching TV, IM'ing with a friend, and heating up some lunch in the microwave. You throw your clothes in the washing machine to do a quick load, hit start, and suddenly—boom—no power.

The first thing to do is figure out if it's just your power that went out—or is the power out in your whole building or neighborhood? If there's a bad storm going on, there's a good chance that's the problem. Look outside to see if your neighbors have lights, or knock on a neighbor's door.

If the problem is just your place, then there are a few possibilities. The outage could be caused by a circuit overload, which happens when you plug in too many things at once. You can usually tell if it's an overload, because the power outage happens right after you start running that last appliance that pushes the limit—the washing machine, iron, hair dryer, or whatever. Window unit air-conditioners are often the big culprits in buildings that aren't wired for a high demand on the electrical system. If the power goes out about 5 or 10 minutes after you've turned on the A/C, that might be the problem.

Before you do anything else, unplug some appliances to cut down on the electrical load. You may also want to call an electrician just to check your place out and make sure it's safe.

In the meantime, getting the power back on is easy if you have a circuit breaker box. Older homes may have fuse boxes which can be dangerous to handle, but renovated homes and buildings have switched to circuit breakers these days. Be prepared by finding out which one you have before there's a problem. Then, if you have circuit breakers, you can grab a flashlight and take the following steps when your power blanks out:

Be prepared by finding out where the circuit breaker box is before there's a problem.

1. Open the little metal gray door to the breaker box and look inside.

If you see a set of switches, like the ones shown here, it's a breaker box. Good. (If you see removable fuses, you'll have to get someone experienced to help you —or call in a professional. Fuses can be dangerous.) The largest switch is your main power. The smaller switches control different branches or areas of your home.

2. Most circuit breakers have three positions— on, off, and tripped.

Tripped is usually in the middle, and it means the circuit was overloaded, so it shut itself off. Look for a tripped switch —a switch that's in a different position from all the others.

3. Turn the tripped switch to the off position.

That's the secret with circuit breakers— you can't turn them back on until you've first turned them off.

4. Then flip the switch back to the on position, and your power should return.

Variations: Some circuit breakers are designed as push buttons instead of switches. You have to push in on the button to turn it on, push in again to turn it off. When tripped, these button-type breakers usually pop out.

If flipping the circuit breaker doesn't do it, or if the power goes out again a few minutes later, the problem could be a short circuit. Shorts are very dangerous wiring situations —it's what happens when there's something wrong with the wiring in one of your walls, outlets, plugs, cords, or appliances. If you can safely turn off the appliance that has the short, do so. But if you have any doubts, your best bet is to call in a professional.

COUGH IT UP:

THE COST OF LIVING ALONE

As exciting as living on your own can be, there's no such thing as a free lunch—or a free apartment, car, cell phone plan, cable hookup . . .

Everything costs money, and once you start paying for it all yourself, the bills can really add up. You can wind up feeling pretty overwhelmed.

Who knew gas and electricity for one month could cost as much as a new coat? Or that car insurance for a year could run you more than a trip to the Bahamas?

You didn't realize that moving out of the house meant giving up your vacations, did you?

Okay, that's the bad news. Unless you've got an exceptionally good job, you're going to have to cut some corners when you're first living on your own. But the good news is that there are a lot of great ways to get by on a budget without giving up the great lifestyle you were dreaming about when you moved out of the house.

Read on!

can I afford that new car?

HOW MUCH DOES IT COST?

Typical living expenses can vary by huge amounts, and the range is affected by an almost endless list of factors—but the main reason why expenses are higher for some people than others is location.

If you live in a major city like Boston, you'll probably be paying more for rent, car insurance, dental work, and dinners out than your friend who lives in a suburban area in the Midwest. (For more details about the cost of living in different parts of the country, visit www.realuguides.com.)

But beyond your zip code, there are a bunch of other factors that could send your bills up or down. Check out the following pages for the lowdown on the most common living expenses. You probably won't have all of these, so just pick out the ones that apply to you.

A BREAKDOWN OF AVERAGE PRICES

EXPENSE	WHY THE RANGE?
RENT/MORTGAGE: FROM $300 TO $2,000 A MONTH	This one's a prime example of why location matters—the high-end rent applies only to the biggest and most expensive cities like New York and San Francisco. You can lower your monthly rent by sharing with roommates. Mortgage payments will vary depending on the interest rate and, of course, the price of the house.
GAS: FROM $20 TO $250 A MONTH	This will depend on whether your apartment is heated with gas or electricity, the climate where you live, the size of your home (it will cost a lot more to heat up a larger space) and also how many of your appliances—like a range or dryer —are fueled by gas. Gas bills will be much higher in the winter, obviously.
ELECTRIC: FROM $30 TO $150 A MONTH	Again, make sure you know whether your rent includes any utilities. Otherwise, you'll shoulder the full cost every time you—for instance—use a blow dryer (a few cents each use), cook in your oven (twenty-five cents an hour), or run your air-conditioner (thirty cents an hour). The air conditioning in particular can really add up.
WATER: FROM $20 TO $60 A MONTH.	If you're a renter, you probably don't pay the water bill—it's usually included in the rent. For homeowners, the range varies depending on how many showers you take, how often you water your lawn, and how many loads of laundry you do. Water bills sometimes include a city or county sewer charge.
GARBAGE COLLECTION: FROM $45 TO $85 A MONTH.	This one's usually only an issue if you're a homeowner. Some cities and towns send a garbage collection bill monthly, quarterly, or annually. Other town don't provide garbage pick-up; you have to hire a private company to haul your trash away.

It's cheaper to live here

PHONE BILL: FROM $25 TO $100 A MONTH

You may not be paying for this at all if you skip the land line and use a cell phone for all your calls. However, you'll need a regular phone if you want Internet access. High phone bills are the result of major long-distance charges.

CELL PHONE BILL: FROM $30 TO $65 A MONTH

You'll pay more for extra prime minutes or a broader calling range. Be careful not to go over your minutes, since the extra charges are usually pretty steep.

INTERNET: FROM $10 TO $50 A MONTH

Using a dial-up modem that connects your computer through your phone line and a low-cost ISP can keep your costs down, but a high-speed DSL or cable Internet connection will cost more.

CABLE OR SATELLITE: FROM $35 TO $75 A MONTH

Lose the premium channels, extra cable boxes, and/or digital service to keep your bill down.

GROCERIES: FROM $200 TO $450 A MONTH

This depends a lot on how much you eat at home and how much you're eating out, plus how savvy you are at bargain shopping. Using coupons can save you anywhere from $5.00 to $30.00 a week. That adds up to between $260 and $1560 per year. At the high end, it's the price of a vacation.

ENTERTAINMENT— MOVIES, DINNERS OUT, PARTIES, ETC.: FROM $75 TO $250 A MONTH

Just one weekend of a movie at the theater, dinner at a restaurant, and coffee and dessert at Starbucks can run you as much as $50.

HEALTH INSURANCE PREMIUM: FROM $150 TO $600 A MONTH

If your job doesn't provide you with health benefits, you'll need to pay for a policy out of pocket. The monthly premium (plus charges not coverd by insurance) could fall anywhere in this range depending on what type of coverage you choose and where you live. (Note that even if you do have health insurance at work, you're probably paying part of that expense as an item deducted from your paycheck.)

RENTERS/HOMEOWNERS INSURANCE: FROM $150 TO $800 A YEAR

Renter's insurance—which covers all of your personal property if you're a renter—is optional, but it's a smart choice to protect your belongings. It's also a lot cheaper than homeowner's insurance, a necessity for homeowners.

HOME MAINTENANCE/ REPAIRS: FROM $100 TO $1500 A YEAR

If you're a renter, you probably don't have to worry about this much—yay!—except for minor fixes. Homeowners should plan for more significant costs, especially if the house is older.

CLOTHING: FROM $300 TO $1000 + A YEAR

This depends a lot on your taste and lifestyle, but it's also affected by where you live and what you do for a living. You'll go through shoes more quickly, and need to buy higher ticket items like boots and heavy down coats, if you live in a cold, snowy climate. You'll run through extra pairs of khakis and white shirts if you work in a restaurant where that's the dress code. Business clothes for an office job are more expensive than jeans.

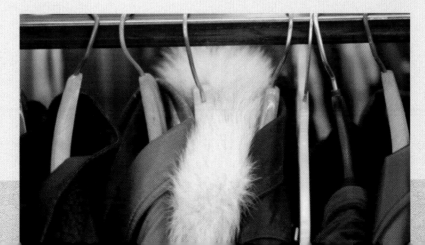

DENTAL:
FROM $50 TO $750 A YEAR

An annual cleaning keeps your smile spiffy without a huge drain on your finances, but if you don't have dental insurance, problems like cavities or root canal work will run you more.

CAR PAYMENTS:
FROM $100 TO $600 A MONTH

If you're paying off a car you've financed—or leasing the car—you'll have monthly payments for more or less depending on how much money you put down and how expensive the car is.

CAR INSURANCE:
FROM $500 TO $2,000 A YEAR

Opting for less complete coverage and higher deductibles are examples of rate-cutting factors you can control. Certain cars are more expensive to insure than others (newer cars, for instance, or SUV's), and your driving history, age, and gender will also affect your rates.

GASOLINE:
FROM $30 TO $80 A MONTH

It's all about commute time, and how often you have to fill up your tank. Gas prices also go up or down depending on various economic factors.

CAR MAINTENANCE/ REPAIRS:
FROM $150 TO $600 A YEAR

Regular oil changes and maintenance won't hit you too hard, but an older car prone to breakdowns can be a real cash-sucker.

BUS/TRAIN COMMUTING:
FROM $0 TO $100 A MONTH

If you have a car, you're probably not using buses or commuter trains. But you might want to consider a switch depending on where you live, since public transportation can be a lot cheaper than using a car!

EXPENSE	WHY THE RANGE?
GYM MEMBERSHIP: FROM $35 TO $75 A MONTH	Fancier gyms will cost more, as will piling on extra benefits like personal trainer sessions.
STUDENT LOANS: FROM $50 TO $150 A MONTH	The good news is, lenders for these types of loans take your income into account when they set your monthly payments, so you shouldn't be too overburdened.
CREDIT CARD BILLS: FROM $15 TO $150 A MONTH	Credit card bills are usually relatively low, but if you've got a lot of them or you've racked up a lot of debt on one or more cards, these can take a sizable chunk out of your paycheck.
VACATIONS: FROM $500 TO $2,500 A YEAR	Is your idea of a vacation a week at a Bahamas resort, or can you live with a weekend car trip to a nearby beach town or big city where you happen to have a friend or relative with a guest room? Vacations are serious money guzzlers, so think hard about how to get away for less.

maybe next year?

HOW TO
MAKE A
BUDGET

You don't need to be
a math whiz to set up
a workable budget.
Just grab a calculator,
dig out a current
pay stub showing your
typical take-home pay, and
follow these 5 easy steps.

1. First figure out your average monthly net salary— your take-home pay.

The number might vary if you're in a job where part of your salary comes from tips, like waitressing, or if you're doing temporary work. Try to take that into account as you figure out your average available cash flow per month.

2. Now add up the average amounts of all of your regular monthly expenses.

(For now, leave out extras like restaurant dinners and movies, and just stick to things like cable/satellite TV and gas and electric bills.) Check the living expenses chart earlier in this chapter for reminders about any costs you may be forgetting. If your total expenses fall well below your monthly take-home pay, excellent! You can jump to step 5. If it's a tight fit, or if the expenses actually come to more, then it's time to look for ways to trim.

3. Before making any heartbreaking decisions about canceling HBO or your Entertainment Weekly subscription, work on ways to save on essentials.

To slash energy and water bills, limit your showers, don't leave faucets running, and set the thermostat (if you have one) at the lowest temperature that allows you to be comfortable in the winter, and the highest in the summer. Remember to adjust it at night when you're sleeping. In the summer, try to get by with open windows and a fan when you can. Turn out lights, don't leave appliances on when you're not using them, and avoid running appliances like a dishwasher or clothes dryer without full loads. Be creative about bills that seem unchangeable—in some states you can lower you car insurance premium by attending a one-day class on defensive driving, for instance, or by using an anti-theft device. Phone companies are always offering new specials; switch to a plan that makes the most sense with your calling habits to avoid hefty long-distance charges. Go through each of your bills and think about how you could cut them down. If you draw a blank, try calling the company and inquiring about possible savings. Don't skimp on anything crucial, like your healthcare, but consider taking smart risks that will lower your bills like opting for a higher deductible if your car is stolen or dropping comprehensive coverage completely on a car with a market value of only a couple thousand dollars.

4. If you still need to trim off more fat to make your expenses fall under your income, it's time to take a look at that EW subscription.

Sorry! Here's where you consider which of your extras you can live without. Cancel any premium cable stations you barely watch; if you rarely watch TV in the first place, think about sticking to basic network stations and saving a larger chunk of change each month. Do you really need the cell phone and the land line? Which do you use more? You might want to drop the home phone and use the cell phone for all your calls.

In some states you can lower you car insurance premium by attending a one-day class on defensive driving.

DO YOU SPEND MORE THAN YOU MAKE?

Monthly Take-Home Pay	$1860.00
Monthly Expenses	$1495.00
Disposable Cash?	$365.00

5. Once you're not overspending your income, you can figure out how to keep it that way.

Do the math to see how much "disposable cash" you have each month—how much is left over after you've paid all your monthly bills. Then make a budget for what you'll need to spend on necessities: food, for instance, or other household goods. Once you have that amount, do your best to stick to it every month, outside of any special circumstances. Help yourself out by using coupons, buying store-brand products if they're cheaper, and stocking up on long-lasting items like canned goods when they're on sale. After you've given yourself a food budget, figure out how much you can spend a month on entertainment costs, and on clothing or other "extra" purchases. Again, once you have those numbers on paper, keep them in mind as the month goes by. Only withdraw what your budget allows from the ATM every week, and don't make any more withdrawals until the following week.

HOW TO

LIVE WITHIN YOUR MEANS AND STILL HAVE FUN

Living on a budget doesn't have to mean a boring life of drudgery. Just try these ideas when you're planning your next weekend's activities.

best fortune cookies!

video night with the girls

MOVIES

GOOD: Look for movie theaters with matinee prices, which often cover movie showings up until 6:00 PM. You can sneak in there with a 5:30 showing instead of the 7:00 you usually go for, and save a few bucks on the ticket price.

BETTER: Save theater movies for the ones that you just can't wait to see, or for blockbuster action flicks that don't work as well on a small screen. Otherwise, stick to renting from a video store.

BEST: Become a member of your local library, where you can usually borrow videos and DVD's for free, as long as you return them in 1-2 days.

DINNER WITH FRIENDS

GOOD: If you're eating out for dinner, try having an appetizer as your entrée, or sharing an entrée with your dinner date.

BETTER: Meet a friend for lunch instead of dinner. Many restaurants offer yummy selections from their dinner menus at lunchtime, at better prices.

BEST: Have some friends over for a pot-luck, in which everyone brings a different part of the meal. That way you're still getting to try dishes you don't have to cook yourself, but you'll save a ton on restaurant costs and tips!

WEEKEND ENTERTAINMENT

GOOD: Find a night club with no cover charge and then make yourself stick to the 2-drink minimum.

BETTER: Don't forget to watch for cool freebies and almost-freebies, like an art gallery opening reception offering wine and cheese, or a local musician playing at a coffeehouse—great entertainment for the price of a couple lattes.

BEST: Get psyched for summertime, when there are tons of free concerts, plays, and other indoor and outdoor events. All you have to do is check a local newspaper for the latest info on what's happening around town.

GROSS VS. NET

For a lot of people, the first glimpse at your paycheck is a major reality check. A $24,000 annual salary doesn't actually mean you'll be bringing home $2,000 a month. Your gross pay will be $2,000 a month, but your net pay—what you can put in the bank—will be significantly lower, because of taxes. Your pay stub will list all the deductions, which should be for local and city taxes, state taxes, and Federal income tax. Also be prepared for Social Security and disability taxes—monies used to fund government benefits for people who are disabled or retired (which would/will include you when and if you fit into one of those categories).

The amount of money that gets taken out of your gross pay is a percentage of your total income, based on a schedule of figures from the IRS about how much tax a person in your situation should pay. The higher your salary, the higher percentage of it you'll owe to Uncle Sam. For instance, a single person filing taxes in 2004 who makes $24,000 would have to pay $715 in income tax, plus 15% of all income over $7,150. But a single person who makes at least $29,050 moves up to the next tax bracket, owing 25% of all income above $29,050. Figures also change for people who are married or have children. The exact numbers can change, so if you want to be certain about which tax bracket you fit into, check the IRS web site at www.irs.gov for up-to-date info.

KNOCK KNOCK:

There's no rule that you have to be best friends with your neighbors, but you never know—you may just find a new friend who lives conveniently nearby.

ALL ABOUT DEALING WITH FAMILY AND FRIENDS

How to make your neighbors love you, your parents leave you alone, and your friends want to hang out at your place all the time.

Sure, you've moved out of the house because you wanted to live on your own. But you didn't mean all alone, all the time, did you? Ideally, you want to find a balance of time to yourself and time with your family and friends. You want to keep your parents at a reasonable distance so you can do the independence thing, without kicking them totally out of your life. And, if you're smart, you want to forge halfway decent relationships with your neighbors.

Plus what's the fun of having your own place if you can't throw a rockin' party every once in a while? Here's a quick look at how to handle relationships with neighbors, family and friends, now that you're living on your own.

great neighbors!

GET TO KNOW YOUR NEIGHBORS

Whether you're the type who's already gearing up for a block party, or someone who likes coming home to some quiet and privacy, knowing at least a neighbor or two is always a good idea. Here are a few reasons why:

1. You get locked out.

Even if you haven't left a spare key with a neighbor (a smart plan), at least you'll have somewhere to go to call your super, landlord, or whoever has the power to reunite you with the inside of your home. You'll also have somewhere to hang out while you're waiting.

2. You have a last-minute need for sugar/butter/ a tape measure/ the entire Frank Sinatra collection on vinyl.

Okay, that last one might be tough, but neighbors can be a huge help when you have one of those cliché moments of realizing you're out of the next ingredient in your recipe, and you don't have time to run to the store. By the way, stopping by to ask for a favor really is a great way to meet your neighbor in the first place, too.

3. You're going out of town.

Maybe you need someone to collect your mail or newspapers, feed your cat, or just keep an eye out and make sure no one suspicious is lingering around your front door. Knowing you have neighbors watching your place while you're away gives you much needed peace of mind.

4. You might actually have some things in common.

There's no rule that you have to be best friends with your neighbors in order to help each other out, but you never know—you may just find a new friend who lives conveniently nearby. Proximity is a huge plus when it comes to those lazy rainy Saturdays when you're lonely for some company, but don't feel like going anywhere.

MEETING NEW PEOPLE

If you're living in a new neighborhood or even a new city or state, you're probably on the prowl for some new friends, too. Aside from getting to know your neighbors, try heading to local hangouts like coffee shops or book-stores, especially if there's a concert or reading given by someone you like. Don't forget about coworkers, since you've already got something major in common. Suggest drinks after work with a big group and see if you click with anyone once you're off the clock.

Also, don't be afraid to ask if anyone you know from your old neck of the woods has other connections where you are now. Set-ups and blind dates aren't just for romance—if you two live in the same town and have a mutual friend or relative, there's a good chance you could hit it off.

SETTING LIMITS WITH PARENTS

Just because you're living on your own doesn't mean your parents will give up that easily—they had a whole lot of time to get used to having you under their roof.

If you feel like they're calling just a few too many times a day—or hour!—or giving you the fifth degree over every choice you make, try out some of these tactics.

look who's here!

1. MAKE A SCHEDULE

Establish a regular day and time for check-in phone calls. If they're still calling a lot for no real reason outside the phone date, let the machine pick up and just say you weren't around.

2. NO SURPRISE VISITS

If your parents live close enough to visit, let them know that surprise "drop-ins" really aren't a good idea since you're so busy and you may not be home. Again, set up scheduled visits so you know when to expect them, and they don't feel excluded from your life.

3. HANDLE IT YOURSELF

Choke back the instinct to call them for advice the second you run into a snag, like if your dishwasher is suddenly on the fritz. Turning to them for help will open the door to a parental invasion. Check with friends, online, and in books (like this one!) first to see if there's an easy solution.

4. SHOW OFF YOUR SUCCESS

Do fill your parents in after you've successfully handled the problem, which will impress them with your responsibility and remind them that you're fine on your own.

Politely but firmly redirect the conversation if they start asking, for instance, where you were when they called first thing Saturday morning. Switch to a topic that features a glaring reminder of your new independence, like a story

STAYING SAFE

There's no foolproof way to avoid being the victim of a crime, but there are definitely ways to slash your risk. Common sense is your best ally. Burn these tips into your brain for extra protection.

1. Make sure doors and windows are locked when you're out or sleeping.

It sounds obvious, but it's easy for an open window or unlocked door to slip your mind, especially if you cracked that window open earlier to let some fresh air in.

2. If possible, install dead bolts on front and back doors.

These work much better than chains to keep unwanted visitors out.

3. Leave lights on when you're not home.

Police say this is the best way to discourage burglars, since most burglars opt for the empty house rather than the occupied one. Leaving lights on makes it look like you're home.

4. Don't hide spare keys in obvious places.

This is probably another no-brainer, but don't give in to the temptation to stick a set of keys in the nearest plant or under the welcome rug. If you feel the need to stash a spare set somewhere besides your car, wallet, or purse (the best options), then leave them with a neighbor who's usually home when you are.

5. Be a mystery on your answering machine.

Don't reveal your name on your outgoing message, and don't change your greeting to let people know if you're going out of town. If you live alone, try not to make that clear either, especially if you're female. Go with something vague like, "No one can answer the phone right now, but please leave your name, number, and a brief message."

6. Don't give out info to "wrong numbers."

If someone calls asking for a person who doesn't live there, say it's the wrong number and end the call there. Never answer a request for your name or for the number that the person dialed.

7. Don't tempt burglars.

As much as possible, keep any expensive belongings like computers or TV's away from doors or windows where they can be easily seen from the outside.

---

about your job, to remind them that you're taking care of yourself now.

5. NO MORE MOOCHING

Avoid borrowing significant funds from your parents if at all possible, since this is another fast-track to giving them a legitimate say in your solo lifestyle.

6. BE FIRM BUT NICE

Welcome (and thank them for) any housekeeping/decorating/etc. input they offer, but be clear about your own ideas. Having alternatives in mind will defuse any potential tension over why you're not taking all their suggestions.

excellent party!

PARTYTIME:
FOUR GREAT EXCUSES TO THROW A PARTY

Has all this talk of cleaning bathrooms, making budgets, and plunging toilets made you forget what's so great about living on your own? Then it's time for a news-flash on one of the best parts—you can have a party whenever you want. Here are some great themes to get you started.

HOUSEWARMING PARTY:

Saving up for some nice sheets, towels, or even a pair of oven mitts? Stop right now. As soon as possible after you've moved in and mostly unpacked, invite everyone over to check out your new place. They'll be psyched to see it, and you'll be psyched at all the household goodies they'll bring as gifts.

ARBOR DAY PARTY:

Pick a holiday, any holiday—as long as it's not one of the headline-grabbers like New Year's or Halloween—and make it your own. Start a tradition that everyone comes to your house to celebrate April Fool's, or President's Day, or good old hug-a-tree Arbor Day.

WINE TASTING PARTY:

Talk about the pinnacle of sophistication—having friends over for a wine-tasting is an excellent way to show off your new digs and hosting skills. Pick up a variety of wines along with some cheese, fruit, and crackers, and invite anyone with a sharp set of taste buds to come join the fun!

BIRTHDAY PARTY:

You can't go wrong with a classic, right? The key is, you probably don't want to do this for your own birthday, when you'd rather relax and let someone else do the work. Try throwing a party for a friend's birthday instead—anything from a cozy dinner for a tight circle of friends, to an all-night blast with whoever can fit in your apartment. If you're planning a major event, have enough on hand to supply each guest with about three drinks. Stock the bar with wine, beer, vodka, rum, and a few different juices and sodas. Just remember that you don't want any drunk driving accidents on your conscience—and in fact, in some states, you can be held legally responsible for someone who gets caught driving drunk after leaving your party—so make sure there are plenty of designated drivers and/or spots in your place for people to crash if necessary.

MORE REAL U...
CHECK OUT THESE OTHER REAL U GUIDES!

YOUR FIRST APARTMENT

Everything you need to know about moving out of the house and into your first apartment, including how to deal with landlords, how to dump your roommate, and much more!

IDENTITY THEFT

Find out how to protect yourself from the #1 crime in the U.S. Includes expert advice about surfing the Internet without leaving a trail for the criminals to follow.

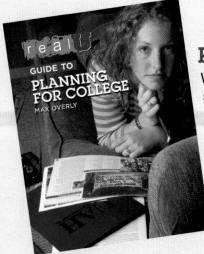

PLANNING FOR COLLEGE

With a timeline for high school freshmen, sophomores, juniors, and seniors, this guide takes you step by step through the whole college selection and application process. Includes a clear and concise overview of financial aid, and much more.

FOR MORE INFORMATION ON THESE AND OTHER REAL U GUIDES, VISIT WWW.REALUGUIDES.COM.